REAL Wealth

A Success Formula

By: Alvaro G. Ramirez III

This book contains information geared toward helping the average person create a financial plan based upon principles determined by the author to be constant across all sections of society. The author makes no guarantee as to your ability to establish your own plan and eliminate your debt. You should always consult with legal counsel when available when dealing with estate planning. You should also consult with a tax advisor when appropriate.

For my beloved wife, Monica. Who even when things were at their darkest stood by my side and loved me unconditionally.

I love you!

Table of Contents

About The Author:

Alvaro Ramirez has been working within the financial industry since 1997. He got into the business because he saw the potential to make lots of money and help people find hope in life. His desire to help people achieve their dreams has led him to create several proprietary programs which have assisted his clients in attaining a peace of mind that otherwise evaded them throughout life. His favorite saying is that he loves to make people cry, but a good cry. He loves to see the pure emotion, which takes over after working with a client who had no hope, and now can see the sun on the horizon as a new day bursts upon their lives.

He started NewLine Consulting in 2002, and he works with consumers and business owners alike providing services from meeting the insurance needs of the client to management and full on business consulting. His insatiable appetite for learning pushes him to consistently research new programs and industry trends, which enables him to help his clients at all stages of life. He believes that America is only as strong as its people, and if debt and insufficient planning weaken its people, then the Country as a whole is weak. He prides himself in his innovation and willingness and ability to think outside the box when it comes to financial planning. This has helped him assist clients who have been told by other planners and consumer credit counselors that there is no hope for them.

He has an MBA in Business Management/Administration but believes that his true worth to his clients comes from his experience in the field and not in the classroom. Although his business has remained small he has helped countless individuals and families realize their dreams. His ability to understand the needs and desires of his clients comes from his own life's experiences. Having grown up poor, and having experienced his own series of financial setbacks, he has viewed it as an educational process that he's gone through to be more in tune with the needs of others. He has taken this knowledge and applied it to creating programs, which are effective in helping his clients.

He writes extensively on Business and issues facing the United States most especially the Constitution of the United States of America. His love for Country, God and Family exceeds anything else in his life and they are truly what define him as a person.

He believes in the human spirit and believes that all people have the ability to achieve greatness if given a chance and if they have desire. The current trend of reliance upon the government concerns him as he sees it as a process of weakening the people and their will to win.

He was the recipient of NRCC Businessman of the Year for the years 2005 and 2006 and received the Ronald Reagan Gold Medal Award for his advancement of Conservative principles in business. In 2012 he received recognition as a business innovator.

He's been invited as the keynote speaker for seminars and has taken time to meet with youth groups to teach them the importance of proper planning from an early age. Because of this, he took time off from business to teach at a small Title I High School where amongst other things he taught Financial Literacy, Economics and Business Mathematics and Personal Finance. Because if his impact on the students he ended up teaching 21 different business courses every school year. The difference that he made was manifest in the appreciation showed by the students.

The information contained within this book has been accumulated over many years of research. He hopes that you find the information useful and beneficial to you and your family.

Chapter One:
Intro: What Is Wealth?

Whenever somebody starts talking about wealth people get excited. It's because when people think of wealth, visions of extravagant vacations, expensive cars and large ornate homes come to mind. Everybody wants to be wealthy but have bought into the mindset that the wealthy get wealthier and the poor get poorer and that the middleclass is disappearing so you either are poor or rich.

This idea and concept of wealth is erroneous, and if you are going to succeed in life and be truly happy with what you achieve, you will need to rethink your definition of wealth. True wealth is not extravagance or riches. The truest definition of wealth is: Having the time to spend doing what you love with those that you love most. That should be the purpose of our lives, not working ourselves to death so that we can have material things that ultimately mean nothing to our families. Wealth is time, quality time; and anybody can be wealthy on literally any income if they are wise and prudent with their finances.

Many financial planners and professionals seek out those who have amassed material wealth because they are paid a commission on a portion of what they get their clients to invest. This leaves the majority of America out in the cold and going to banks to find help. We will discuss the pitfalls associated with this practice later in this book, and I will give you a hint, it's not a good practice.

As you read through the following chapters you will be educated on what I call the Financial Success formula. I've put together this program over the past 16 plus years. You may recognize many of them because they are nothing new. The difference is that you will not only know what they are, but you will know how they work and how to implement them in your own life and begin to create true wealth for you and your family.

Before you continue with your reading you will need to start changing your mindset. You need to believe that wealth is possible, and that you can be wealthy. It won't be easy, nothing important ever is. The steps are easy enough, but it takes a discipline that most people are afraid to try. Depending on your situation and income level you may feel what some of my clients have called pain, but rest assured the pain won't last forever, and once you've mastered the seven steps you will be stronger for having done so.

It's time to start thinking outside of the box. Make a commitment now to do it for not only yourself, but for your family, for those that you love and that love you in return. Remember financial strain is the leading cause of divorce, people allow the stress and strain that is inherent with financial difficulty to rip apart their relationship with the one that they love, thus hurting the entire family and ultimately the society— as a whole.

The financial epidemic that is facing America and much of the civilized world today is serious. If this epidemic were a disease, the governments of nations would be clamoring to stop the tide before it reached pandemic proportions. In our own country our government passes laws penalizing the credit card companies, mortgage companies, financial institutions, businesses, etc., trying to fix it for the American people. More laws and legislation are not what is needed, but education. We must believe that people are inherently intelligent. That each person who is born into this world is endowed by his or her Creator with certain abilities; and it is society, and to a point government interference, that perpetuates the problem.

I recently took a three-year hiatus from business and taught Business and Financial Literacy at a struggling High School in a small community. For every single one of these students (Juniors and Seniors), it was the first time that they had heard anything about how personal finance really worked. I was able to use real world examples to drive home the lessons being taught. As a financial professional it was a rewarding experience to make a difference in the lives of these young men and women. Education at a young age is essential to the overall success of an individual. I applaud the State of Utah for its preemptive move in making Financial Literacy a required class for graduation.

It is essential for us to understand here in The United States of America that The Constitution does not guarantee financial success, but rather allows for the creation an environment where if desired the Citizen can obtain such success with hard work and determination. The "American

Dream" is not dead; it lives in the hearts of every individual who desires something more. Now is the time to take this dream, create a vision in your heart and mind and make a plan that will allow you to achieve your dreams and experience the feeling of freedom that true wealth brings to those who are able to achieve it in this lifetime.

To get started you will need to sit down with your spouse or loved ones and discuss your goals and aspirations. Mutual understanding and commonality in your goals and desires is crucial to your success. If the both of you are working towards different goals and outcomes you will find yourself drifting apart and your plan will fail. Make a list of those things that you would like to do and what is needed to do them. It is important to be reasonable but make them challenging.

 Begin by planning on how you will achieve these goals and map out the steps that you will need to take to do so. Put it down on paper, if it is not written down, it's just a dream, and you need a vision, not another dream.

Take those most important elements that represent your vision and create a vision board. Hang this vision board somewhere in your home where you will see it daily at least once if not more. Place the carrot in front of you and let it lead you to success.

As I mentioned earlier, I took a small break from business and taught High School business classes. One of these classes was a leadership principles class in which we created vision boards. I had a student come up to me at the end of my last school year teaching and tell me she had hung her vision board in her room and that she looks at it every day. She said that it is helping her focus on her goals and that she was doing better because of it.

I thought to myself, here's a young lady who never once thought about her future, and now was focused on it, and was determined to succeed. Vision boards are powerful, I cannot stress it enough. Create a vision board, look at it daily, and see your life change to reflect the board and your vision.

I always suggest creating goals in four principle categories. These categories are; career, personal, family/relationships, and spiritual. By focusing your efforts or goals in these four areas you will ensure a balanced life. Many times we focus on only one aspect of our lives and we forget the truly important areas. Dr. Stephen R. Covey consistently speaks of balance in your life. In his Seven-Habits he outlines in habit number seven the necessity of preserving self. In my estimation ensuring that you are working on every aspect of your life simultaneously does this.

Spiritual:

Many times, we get caught up in life and forget that human beings are essentially spiritual beings. We would never consider for a moment starving ourselves or denying ourselves of sustenance on a daily basis. Yet we do just that to that spiritual being which lies within each of us. We work so hard at isolating ourselves from spirituality that in essence we reach a point of spiritual death, meaning that we withhold spiritual nutrients from ourselves until that light which is inherent in each of us flickers into non-existence.

Setting a spiritual goal can be as easy as saying that we will start attending weakly church services and can blossom into reading the scriptures daily. I recently read an article in a trade publication for financial professionals where a gentleman was giving his formula for success in business. He started by pointing out that he like many men and women in the business world started his career with one object in mind becoming the best and dominating his market. He worked long hours and eventually started working on Sunday because he had to have the added advantage over his competition. He went on to say that for a while this worked, until one day he woke up and realized that something was missing in his life. His family relationship was wavering, his health was declining, and his mental focus was suffering. He started to take a look at his life and realized that he had completely starved his spiritual self until he had distanced himself from religion in its entirety. He made a commitment to start attending church meetings and not working on Sunday. He said within a short amount of time he realized that this was making all the difference. He was happier, his family was stronger, and his business exploded. He mentioned that he had been doing that for 50 years at the publishing of the article and wanted to warn new producers to avoid the pitfall of falling into the trap to neglect the spiritual self.

I have a good friend who has taught me a lot about not sacrificing spirituality for business success. His business remains relatively small, but he is always ready to serve his fellow men. He is blessed with a healthy family and a strong marriage because of this. Basically, what I am saying is that in order to obtain true success and happiness one must feed their spiritual self, through worship, service, and faith. All religions teach these principles; they aren't relegated solely to Christians. Proper balance is essential to a healthy psyche.

Career:

We are talking about financial success; therefore, it is essential to set defined goals with regards to your career. Consider the following questions, among others:

What do you want to achieve in your career?

Do you want to train for a new career?

What is going to motivate you and push you to succeed?

These are questions that you must ask yourself when you sit down and discuss the setting of goals in this area of your life. Many people want so badly to start a business and be self-employed, but never set a plan on how they are going to do so. As a business planner I meet with lots of people who tell me that their dream has always been to start the particular business that they are speaking to me about, but when we get into the particulars of the business, it becomes obvious that they've done no planning on how or why.

Others who work for the same organization for their entire life, never set goals on how to advance in the organization and just wait for their turn to eventually come up, all the while watching others who have been working there for a shorter amount of time be promoted over them.

If you want to succeed financially and be happy you must set goals for your career. These goals cannot be generic. I've seen goals like, "be promoted to management by the end of the year". When asked how, there is no answer. If you do have a goal to be promoted, what are you doing to prepare, or deserve the promotion? Your goals must have milestones attached to them, meaning defined objectives upon which you can gauge the successful completion or progression towards completion.

If you're object is to get a promotion start with setting goals within your current area of responsibility. Plan to improve yourself in your current position, which will cause others to take notice and eventually give you that promotion that you desire. Career goals are often difficult because we often feel that our career outcome is out of our hands. This is an erroneous belief and it must be cast out of your mind and heart. You must believe that your future is in your hands, and not in the hands of another.

Personal:

You are no good to yourself, your employer, or your family if you are not happy with yourself. The setting of personal goals varies from individual to individual. They can range from reading a new book to losing weight. They've got to challenge you and improve you.

For instance, I typically have a goal to learn something new. I spend a lot of time researching new topics and activities. I have an insatiable appetite to learn and grow my mind. People have often made fun of me because I tend to read textbooks for enjoyment. I've taught myself things like web development and computer programming. On the flip side I know a gentleman who absolutely hates to read or do anything beyond what he needs to do to get by. His ignorance is baffling within the industry that he has chosen to work in and other areas of knowledge. I am not saying that you must learn everything and know everything, but you should have a personal goal to improve your knowledge. Your brain is a muscle and needs to be worked out daily. As such if you don't exercise it, the brain begins to atrophy, and it becomes more difficult later on to learn new things.

If you have a personal goal is to lose weight, ask yourself "why?". Have a clear objective in mind for your goal. With the weight issue, is it to improve health, or maybe to feel better about yourself, or is it some other reason? Think about your objective and set your milestones toward that objective. It helps to set up a reward system for those goals that you achieve. The rewards do not need to be major, but they should motivate you to finish out the course and complete your goal. For example, if you lose weight, maybe you would like to buy yourself a new outfit.

Just remember, when you are setting your personal goals you need to challenge yourself and the outcome should be an improvement of you as a person.

Family/Relationships:

My mantra has always been, "don't build your business at the expense of your family." I borrowed it from Walt Disney, and it comes from a book that I read on him when I was ten years old. A lot of times we go through life building friendships and relationships with others while we neglect our families. We would never yell at or threaten to hit a co-worker who has spoken to us in a flippant manner, but that is what we do with those in our families. We don't worry about ruining the relationship we have with our spouses or children but work hard at maintaining our friendships outside of the home.

When we set goals within the area of family and relationships we need decide what it is that we want for our family. Sometimes these goals can be as simple as a family vacation, or as complex as regaining the respect of our spouse and children. If the latter is your objective, I suggest that you start your process by asking for forgiveness from those you have offended with your actions. Asking for forgiveness is powerful. It shows those that we've offended that we have humbled ourselves and set aside our pride enough to recognize that we were wrong and that the way that we treated them was inappropriate.

Your success in life's endeavors will greatly rest upon your ability to effectively establish and maintain your relationships with your family members and others with whom you interact on a daily basis.

These goals are essential to your success. When times get tough, and I can guarantee you that they will, you can review them and see that there is a reason behind it all. Like an airplane traveling across the globe needs to constantly make course corrections in order to stay on target, you too will need to consistently make corrections in your course so that you don't deviate from your objective and slip back into your old ways that you are trying to overcome. The afore mentioned vision board will aide you in this.

A true financial plan is a "living" document. Life is fluid and unforeseen obstacles can tend to appear out of nowhere. Too many financial consultants leave their clients to fend for themselves (unless there are a great amount of assets under management) once a plan is prepared.

Today in America everyone has a friend, brother, son, uncle, etc who considers themselves a financial consultant, when all they are, are people who took a test and joined the Amway of financial services. They learn to punch numbers in a computer and the software spits out a document that they call a customized financial plan and they leave it at that. These "customized plans" fail to recognize that things can change at the blink of an eye and the plan is obsolete and useless.

Your traditional producer is out there and for the most part practicing five years of one year's training. The average agent sticks it out about 3 years and bails, leaving his or her clients orphans in the financial world. Producers who inherent these clients neglect to contact them on a regular basis, and they are lost somewhere between cracks. Let's face it, unless you have a net worth, which permits the producer to advance his, or her own financial agenda or plan you are not important in their minds. This is a fact of life in the financial industry. There are not that many altruistic producers putting aside their goals to help someone else achieve theirs if it doesn't advance their career.

Consumers not only have to watch out for these pseudo-consultants, but they need to look out for scams as well. Just the other day I heard an advertisement on the radio for a debt elimination program that claimed to teach you how to pay off a 30-year mortgage in two years, which is impossible unless the mortgage was already near term or the individual client had a substantial income.

I've heard of programs which guarantee you financial freedom by placing your home into interest only style mortgages and which get you to "invest" the difference in payment into some investment strategy where they show large returns which allows you to pay off your home in a pre-determined amount of years with the excess funds found in these investments.

You have agents having their clients put all excess or discretionary funds into insurance policies promising them that they can use the cash value as retirement income. The list goes on.

There is no lack of ingenuity when it comes to getting your money from you, which is why it is important that you learn the necessary steps and become an educated consumer. By approaching financial planning in this light, you can easily identify any program, which may harm you financially.

By the end of your reading of this book you will feel confident in your ability to establish a solid plan with the assistance of a financial professional who will assist you in implementing some of the suggestions given in the various chapters and who will identify those financial vehicles which will best benefit you in your needs. You then will be able to maintain the plan and make the necessary adjustments when necessary, thus taking control of your future and leaving nothing to chance.

Chapter Two:
Step One: Increase your Income/Cash Flow

Whenever I start talking to my clients about increasing their cash flow I can see the question in their face. "Is this guy nuts? He wants me to increase what I bring home?" And the answer is always yes; I do expect you to start bringing into your household more money. It is essential for you to increase your income to secure a stronger hold of your finances. If you have excessive debt or are always feeling the pressure of finances, it's because you don't bring enough home in income, therefore to get on top you need to increase your income. Remember you are in the state that you are in because you either are a very poor money manager or don't bring enough home. Let's assume the latter rather than the former.

Now this doesn't necessarily mean that you must go out and get a second or even in some cases a third job, but you do have to make some adjustments to increase your discretionary income. For every ten dollars you add to your income you increase your potential to succeed in implementing a strong and balanced budget, which will enable you to reach your objectives outlined in chapter one. Remember those goals that we talked about and that vision? You should have your vision board in front of you while reading this book to remind you why you are even interested in finding out about this program. If your dreams and vision don't require you to have more discretionary income you probably didn't challenge yourself enough and you need to review and revise your goals.

How can you increase your income without going out and getting another job? Well one of the easiest ways is to review your annual taxes that you file with the IRS. Do you typically get a tax return? How much is it? Are you comfortable with giving an interest free loan to the federal government every year? If you get a tax return every year your first step to take is to ascertain an annual average taking the amount for the past 3 years.

> **_Example:_** *Bill and Mary received a tax return of $3,500 last year. The year before their return totaled $4,000, and the year before that their return was $3,000. To determine the average, they would take the sum of the years and divide it by 3. This gives them a rough average of their annual tax return.*

$$\$3,500$$
$$\$4,000$$
$$+\$3,000$$
$$\$10,500 / 3 = \textbf{\$3,500}$$

Now that you have your average you can go to your Human Resources Department where you work and ask to have your Allowances changed on your Federal Form W-4. Make sure that you only change it enough to ensure that over the course of the year you will pay the amount that you averaged out. It does you no good if you end up having to pay additional taxes and you don't have the money to do so. If we use the example above, Bill and Mary would be bringing home an additional $30 to $75 per month depending on their total income and their Adjusted Gross Income claimed on their filed taxes. As a disclaimer, if you have a tax adviser that you typically work with, I would advise you to consult with them. They know what they are doing when they prepare your taxes and they should be able to assist you with making the right decision when it comes to minimizing your taxation. This is something that they should already be doing with you. If your tax adviser has never talked to you about taxation minimization, I would suggest that you find yourself another person to work on your taxes.

Another action that you can take to increase your cash flow is to check how your payroll deductions are made for your insurance premiums. Are they taken out before taxes? Many companies fail to do this because they erroneously believe that it would be too difficult to take them pre-taxed or they don't know that they can. There is a Section 125 POP (Premium Only Plan), which enables employees to pay their share of health insurance costs on a pre-tax basis. By paying your premiums pre-taxed you now have less taxes being taken out of your paycheck, thus once again increasing your monthly cash flow. If you work for a large corporation, they most likely already do this. You must understand corporate tax laws. Companies have to match your taxes that you pay, therefore, if they can reduce your tax responsibility they in turn reduce theirs.

Of course, these tactics wouldn't be beneficial if you didn't get an IRS tax return when you filed your taxes. What do you do then? Well, what I usually would suggest is that the client start looking for different employment. Put together a strong resume, which highlights your strengths and the experience that you have. If you do not have a strong employment history you may need to produce a resume which highlights your strengths, and which outlines your life experience, followed by your employment history. This will give the potential employer a look into your potential. This would mean that you would need to highlight any leadership experience that you might have had in the past. For example, if you were a Student Body Officer while in school, or maybe you were in the Boy Scouts and were a leader in your troop. Look for ways to highlight those qualities that are being sought after to fill the position. If you need to you might have to consider going back to school and securing a degree. Meet with an employment counselor and see what you can do to more effectively promote yourself. Attend professional networking meetings and sell yourself to business owners and employers who may be present. There are options for you if you are willing to take the initiative and grab hold of your destiny.

In most cases I try to move away from having to hold more than one job. The reason why, is that in my estimation, family is very important and time spent with your family should be paramount in your life. Working two jobs is anathema to this belief; in that it greatly dilutes the time available to spend with your family. I do concede that there are some occasions in which this is necessary, but this should be a temporary fix and not a permanent solution to the cash flow dilemma.

Another method that we use to increase your cash flow is by taking ownership of your current job. This means that you no longer view it as a burden that is sucking the very life from you. You make the conscience decision right now that from this point on when you walk into your place of employment you will epitomize happiness and self-confidence.

How many times have you gone to work and as soon as you walk into your place of employment all semblances of joy that you may have had prior disappear and someone asks how you are doing and you retort, "I'm here aren't I?" I've seen people who look as if they were just sentenced to 23 years hard labor for a crime that they didn't commit.

Taking ownership means that you will accept that you have a job to do and that your family depends upon you doing exceptionally well at it. Go above and beyond what is expected of you and stand out. Don't be ashamed of what others might say; they aren't the ones responsible for providing for your family, **you** are. Make the management team take notice of you, and when evaluations come around the likelihood that you will receive high marks on your performance are greater, and therefore a greater raise will be extended. This method takes a bit longer to realize an increase in cash flow but nonetheless produces one. Remember it just takes an additional $10 to make a difference. Who knows, you might even make enough of an impact on the management team where they will approach you about a promotion.

I had a job once as a Regional Manager for a cleaning company. The pay was okay, it covered my needs at the time, but just the needs. I was worth more to the company, but they couldn't afford to pay me. I went in and worked hard every day. My efforts grew the region 20% every month. One day I was sitting in my home thinking about our situation. I felt discouraged as I looked around me. I had a large family of 7 living in a town house apartment that was about 1,000 square feet total. It was tight. I looked over the budget and thought to myself that if I ever was going to move out of the situation I needed to make more money.

I went into work the following Monday and informed the Senior Vice President that I was leaving unless they gave me more money. She asked what I needed, and I told her the amount that I had determined that we needed to move into a bigger place. The amount that I gave her represented an increase of about 45% from what I was then earning. She told me not to make a move until she got back to me, and that she would be back in touch before the end of the day. Within an hour she was in my office offering me what I requested.

It was as simple as making myself too valuable of a commodity to give up. Anybody can do the same thing, you just have to believe in yourself and have the confidence that you are the most valuable asset your employer has.

Another way for you to increase your monthly cash flow is to start a part-time business from your home. I'm not saying to go sign up to start selling soap and vitamins to everyone you know, unless that is something that interests you. There are lots of things that you can do.

For example, many people make money by selling items on eBay. I know of a gentleman who sold a pair of his old socks with his signature for $10 (remember $10 is all you need to make a difference). Another example is from an associate of mine. He had a client who would go to garage sales and spend about $25 and turn around and sell it on eBay and make on an average of $2,000 per month. I am not saying that you have to start being an eBay merchant to make money; there are a lot of people who have never made a dime on eBay.

You can also look at your hobbies and see if they can be turned into cash flow instruments for your family. In my case I've set it up so that in essence everything that I love has become a tax write off for me and produces an income stream into my home.

For example, I love working with wood and building custom furniture, so I started a company called The Wooden Box Company, which produces a small income for my family and gives me an opportunity to earn extra money doing something that I love. It also gives me a chance to work with my oldest son and teach him the art of working with wood.

Find something in your life that you love and see about turning it into an income source. You never know it might even take over your current income and become your only income source.

I want to return for a moment to a comment that I made a couple of paragraphs up about selling soap and vitamins. I was referring to the Direct Sales Industry. I believe that the Direct Sales Industry has a ton of power when it comes to making ordinary everyday people into millionaires. It is hard work, but if you are disciplined enough and want it bad enough you can make money and live the lifestyle that you truly desire.

The trick is to find the right company. This is the difficult task because there are a lot of companies that are just in it to make the money and really don't care about the associate who has come into the company wide eyed and full of dreams. I completely endorse this method of increased cash flow with the caveat that you must look for the right company and do your research.

Make sure that the company's vision and mission match your life's mission and vision. Make sure that the company's compensation plan allows you to make what you need to make. A lot of companies are not set up to provide adequate compensation for the person who just wants to come in and sell some products and not really build a team. So just do your research and due diligence and you will do fine.

The point is that you need to think of something and then do it. If we allow ourselves to believe that it can't be done, we won't do it and we will continue to fail and life will seem dismal and not worth the effort. But I guarantee you that life is worth it; believe me, when life gets darkest you need to keep pushing forward. I suggest prayer in this case to all my clients. When life gets out of hand go to the source of peace. Sometime all that is needed is proper money management, which we will get into in the next chapter.

Chapter Three: Step Two: Learn To Manage Your Money So That It Doesn't Manage You. Eliminate Debt

Proper money management is crucial to your success. We hear the adage of living from paycheck to paycheck and we think it indicative of what life is, basically, getting a Master's Degree from the School of Hard Knocks, and graduating at the top of your class. Is this necessary? Is this what life's all about? In my personal opinion I believe that life is meant to be more, but more and more it is no longer living from paycheck to paycheck but living from payday loan to payday loan.

I can hear you saying, "but we have a budget and we still can't seem to get a handle on our financial situation". If this is you, go back and read chapter two then proceed with this chapter. Too many people go through life on a wing and a prayer, but too often forget the prayer. Managing your financial resources is a full-time job, which takes a great deal of discipline.

If you would indulge me for a moment I would like to sing the praises of one of the best modern-day budgeters that I know of. As a matter of fact, I think that she could do better at balancing the federal budget than any politician in Washington DC. This person of whom I speak is my beloved wife. She oversees the managing the finances for our home; she creates the budget monthly, plans our expenses, and ensures that every month there is a proper and balanced budget. Being self-employed has not always been easy and at times funds have been scarce, but she has been able to ensure financial solvency through tough times and it has made us both stronger. She is my hero! Nobody can hold a candle to her skill. I might be paid to develop financial plans for individuals and companies, but she is the best at what she does.

How is this accomplished? Well, the first thing that you must get into your mind is that your family is and should be your principle venture that you are expecting to see succeed. Just like most businesses fail within the first five years due to financial insolvency, so do many families fail within the same time period because of the same circumstances.

Let's take the example of a new business starting out. The excitement is high, and expectations are equally as high. Visions of monetary success run rampant in your mind's eye, and it is just a matter of time and you will be flying in your personal jet to some undisclosed location for the weekend.

You start out with purchasing the needed equipment, and of course the best will only do because your customers, friends and family need to perceive success when they see you. And of course, the business is going to succeed so you begin spending future revenues by taking draws on the cash reserves of the company to purchase a new vehicle and house for your family. You do your advertising, and you even go as far as putting together a website to promote your business online. You're set, success is in the bag; or is it? The first few months' sales are rather scarce, but of course you thought of this prior to opening your doors and planned enough reserves to maintain the company through these slow times.

Finally, things start picking up and you are "succeeding", you begin taking bigger draws and spending more money because it is the fruit of your labors. Then as what happens in every industry you hit a slow period, all markets are cyclical and fluctuate all the time. You realize that you don't have enough reserves in the bank and you begin using your credit cards and extending yourself with more credit accounts to pull yourself through.

You now cycle out of it and sales begin to increase, but now you have higher debt ratios than you previously did. Not only do you have your regular expenses, but you also have additional debts that you must satisfy along with everything else. You maintain these debts and you cycle back into a slow time and add even more debt to the already overloaded debt load being held and maintained by your company.

Your ability to maintain your personal income is strained and you begin to start coming apart. Soon the only remedy that you can see through the murky waters of debt is bankruptcy and declaring your business insolvent. Your business fails, and you are left scratching your head and wondering why and how this could have happened.

The same scenario occurs with families. Two people meet and decide that they love each other and that they want to start a family. The young man is madly in love and wants his love to be reflected in the ring that he chooses for his bride to be. He runs to the local jewelry store and finds the most beautiful ring, and what a steal at only $45 a month, and he buys it. They get married, and since everything must be done just right they get a small loan to help pay for the reception, and everything is cool and copasetic.

After a small period of living in an apartment and hearing their friends say that renting is the equivalent to throwing your money away, they decide to purchase a home, and since mom and dad had a nice home and everything was ok with them they must have the same thing. They buy a nice beautiful home and since the neighbors all have nice new cars, they feel that it would probably be prudent to go and get a new car for themselves as well, since the commercial says that they can get one for only $250 a month.

Now what about furniture? That nice new home looks awfully bare, so they go out and purchase a house full of furniture on of course, credit. They know that as soon as they are finished with school a better job will come along and they can get it paid for in no time at all.

Things seem to be going well and the stork makes a visit and they have a beautiful baby. They find themselves having to get the needed supplies and they put it on the credit card. Now, they must decide what to do. Is the new mother going to stay home with the baby or continue to work? They look over the budget and see that her continued employment is needed because the father still needs time to finish school. The mother goes back to work and finds a daycare to take care of the new baby.

This new situation creates a new dilemma for this young family, why is there less money to be able to satisfy the monthly expenses? They continue to press through and find themselves having to put more and more on credit. They refinance the home to tap into equity that has built up and pay for the car. Now, they've freed up some additional money and decide that a bigger vehicle is needed because of the baby and purchase another vehicle. This continues and the debt to income ratio increases, until one day in disgust and confusion they begin to blame each one the other for the debt problems that the family is facing. They decide that they no longer love each other and plan a divorce. They have declared their family bankrupt and insolvent.

It's unfortunate, but this scenario plays itself out in one form or another with slight variations every day and it is tearing apart our families and weakening society. As I mentioned in Chapter One, our propensity for acquiring debt in America is ruining our Country. Debt is a form of bondage, and the mere definition of bondage is the absence of freedom.

We've done a great disservice to our children in that we've taught them that immediate gratification is good, and that we should not burden ourselves with waiting for those things that we need. Many social economists believe that this phenomenon is a product of Capitalism and a Free Market system. They believe that Capitalism breeds greed and excessivism. This couldn't be further from the truth.

The product of Capitalism is freedom; freedom to choose the financial path that you decide, and not one that is chosen for you. Human nature produces greed, and this vice runs rampant in all economic models. But I regress, and this in and of itself is a topic for a book of its own.

As an Economics teacher, I would spend a week teaching the various economic models that are in utilization today describing the ins and outs of each model. My students would always come to the conclusion that Capitalism is not the evil pariah it is made out to be, but rather the catalyst for freedom and success that it is designed to be.

Now, Consumerism is a different beast altogether. Consumerism does breed greed and excessivism, but it is not a by-product of Capitalism, but rather human weakness.

Let's discuss a method in which you can manage your finances and eliminate your debt without increasing your monthly outlay. We are going to return for a moment to the analogy of a business.

Every successful business produces a monthly forecast of expenses and income for the upcoming month. This forecast assists the business in preparing itself financially to ensure that there are adequate funds in place to cover expenses and that there is a plan for revenues needed during the course of the month. I teach each one of my clients that in order to succeed financially they need to start treating their family's financial resources in the same manner that a business treats its resources. Treat your money like a business, following the path laid out by every successful business throughout time. Success doesn't just happen because you wish really hard for it, it is planned and prepared for.

Forecasting your finances or your budget is quite simple. Although similar in concept to a budget a forecast is a little different. A forecast is a living document that recognizes that life is constantly changing. Too many people make a budget as part of their New Year's resolutions and end up falling away from it shortly after the New Year because they can't follow it.

 A proper forecast is prepared at the close of a month to make ready for the upcoming month. The first step in preparing one is that you must review all expenses for the concluding month, and break them down into their individual "expense accounts", for example groceries, fuel, car payments, etc.

Once you've determined the expense amounts and categorized them, you must prepare a ledger in which you assign a dollar amount to each account. Add all the forecasted amounts and determine what is needed to break-even for the month, you are planning on equilibrium in your budgeted forecast. Now you know exactly what is needed to ensure that by month end you will retain financial solvency.

If done properly you will see exactly where your money goes every month and you should be able to create what is known as a margin, which will be used in the next step involved with properly managing your money. I've created a program that I typically provide for my clients which tracks in real-time their expenses and income and gives them a snapshot picture of what it looks like.

It is beneficial to monitor your daily expenses so that you can ensure that you are remaining true to your forecasted budget. The program that I referenced that I provide my clients with prepares a pie graph and gives them the ability to see in real time the allocation of funds. I always teach sales teams that 75% of people are visual rather than audio in nature. That means more people respond to a visual stimulus rather than just reading or hearing information. That is why we always provide pictorial representations for our clients.

Let's step back for a moment to discuss the before mentioned margin. You may be asking yourself at this point what is a margin. The answer simply put is money identified as "discretionary" income. Many times, once we've put eyes to the budget and identified where our money is being spent we can identify a portion that is being wasted and can be pulled out. This portion of money will be your key to taking care of debt. You must be creative at times to create this margin, but it can be done.

Remember our objective is to create wealth, and you can't create wealth while maintaining debt. It's like pumping air into an inflatable raft with a whole in it. Once we've created the margin, we need to now look at preparing a debt elimination program that will eliminate the debt in as short amount of time as possible.

Now, this is where the pain and discipline come into play. You are going to have to really want to succeed if you are going to be aggressive enough to eliminate your debt not merely maintenance it. Are you willing to sell your home, your cars, boats, ATV's, etc., to make this work? Are you willing to maintain a strict budget/forecast and not deviate from it? It's time for the rubber to hit the road, and for you to take the wheel and chart your own course in life.

The first thing that you need to do is make a list of all your debts. Be sure to include your balances, minimum payments (not what you usually pay), interest rates, and the estimated payoff date. Sort these debts so that the highest interest rates are at the top. You will need to assign the margin that you created during the forecast portion of this step, to an account. Most of the time the rule of thumb is to assign it to the account that charges the most in interest, but this is not always the case. And since I can't go into every scenario possible it will have to suffice to say that the best thing to do is to assign it to the account with the lowest balance, this will enable you to move more rapidly through your debts.

A	B	C	D	E	F	G	H	I	J	K
CURRENT OUTLOOK										
INCOME:	PRE-TAX:									
	POST-TAX:	$3,806.12								
DEBT SCHEDULE AS CURRENTLY EXECUTED:										
CATAGORY	PAYMENT		BALANCE		TYPE		INTEREST RATE		PROJECTED PAY OI	
Chase	$161.00		$3,591.63		CC		29.99		2.75 years	
HOUSE PAYMENT	$889.29		$118,009.43		MORTGAGE		5.75			
HELOC	$114.64		$14,346.42		Equity Line		10.5			
Chase MK	$101.00		$3,828.04		CC		29.99		10 years	
Discover	$174.00		$7,056.25		CC		27.49		9.5 years	
MBNA	$286.00		$9,611.43		CC		19.98		4.13years	
Car	$237.75		$6,700.86		Loan		9.9			
QWEST	$47.18				UTIL					
UTAH POWER	$90.00				UTIL					
QUESTAR	$70.00				UTIL					
TAY-BEN (WATER)	$50.00				UTIL					
Prescriptions	$40.00									
Groceries	$500.00									
School Lunches	$50.00									
Fuel	$250.00									
Misc. Spending	$542.68									
Comcast	$56.19									
Verizon	$44.59									

Once the margin is assigned you will add it to the already budgeted/forecasted payment. Once that debt is paid you will roll the entire payment over to the next account and so on until you are completely debt free. Sounds simple? Well it is, but for some reason most people fail and give up within the first few months. Because they can't stick to it, and there is no discipline or firm desire in their hearts to get it done. When I create a custom plan for clients I work the numbers to move through the debts as fast as possible. There are a number of ways to do this, and once again, I am unable to show every conceivable way of establishing your debt elimination strategy.

The next portion, of managing your debt is setting up your mortgage so that your payments are most effective. When a mortgage is amortized at inception; the payment is determined on the variables involved like the interest rate and term of the loan. By making your payments on time you ensure that in 30 years your loan will have been paid off, and there is nothing wrong with this. Did you ever look at the Good Faith Estimate when you closed on your loan? Do you know how much you are paying for your home when everything is said and done?

Most people just glance over it, because there is nothing that can be done about it and if you want to own a home you have to be willing to pay the price. But what price are you willing to pay? There is a legal and easy way to set up your loan so that it can be paid off in as little as 7 years and in turn save yourself literally hundreds of thousands of dollars in interest.

What you need to do is contact your mortgage holder and inform them that you want to organize a bi-monthly payment schedule on your mortgage. They will require you to make an initial double payment, which can be done if you are still getting a tax return or through another method, either through your savings or a loan from your 401k, or something similar. The point is you will need to get the double payment ready for the mortgage company. Once this occurs your normal payment will be split in two portions, which will be due at the beginning and middle of the month. The way this works is that you are now paying less interest because the principle is being paid off in shorter increments, the interest is not accruing on a full month. Therefore, more of the payment is applied to the principle balance of the mortgage thereby saving you money. The typical 30-year loan will be paid off within 7 years using this method.

The reason why most mortgage companies don't readily offer this as an option to their debtors is because they lose money on the mortgage investment by doing so. If your mortgage holder informs you that they don't have this type of program available, you may look into refinancing your home with a mortgage company that does and set up the payment method right at inception, you may be able to roll your double payment into the refinance.

No matter what you do, never refinance your home to pay off debt. There are too many companies and so-called financial consultants who say that they will get you out of debt, but all they are, are loan officers in disguise. Any fool can consolidate several smaller bills into one large one, but all that does is mask the problem and puts your debt into a 30-year payoff. The tax incentives are nice, but what is more important, tax savings or freedom from debt? You need real relief, therefore be aggressive and eliminate the debt that you have from your life, and if you do this you will be able to remain debt free forever because you will have learned many valuable lessons and will have taught yourself that you can do it. If you want to consolidate your debt go ahead and do so but take the same dollar amount that you were paying previously and make that payment to your loan. You must make the move which makes the most sense for you and your family, and only you can make that decision, nobody else can or ought to try and make it for you.

Writing a book on this subject is always difficult, and too many writers make blanket statements and present it in a way that makes it sound as if that is the only way and you have no choice. I take the opposite position. There are so many variables involved when it comes to a family's finances that the individual invested in the situation the most must make the decision and stick with the decision. I believe in your ability to make correct choices, and if it turns out not to be the correct choice change your position and move forward having learned from your mistakes. No matter what, never give up if you think that you failed, because if you don't give up, in essence you never failed. One of my favorite quotes of all time comes from Teddy Roosevelt in which he says:

"It is not the critic who counts; not the man who points out how the strong man stumbles, or where the doer of deeds could have done them better. The credit belongs to the man who is actually in the arena, whose face is marred by dust and sweat and blood, who strives valiantly; who errs and comes short again and again; because there is not effort without error and shortcomings; but who does actually strive to do the deed; who knows the great enthusiasm, the great devotion, who spends himself in a worthy cause, who at the best knows in the end the triumph of high achievement and who at the worst, if he fails, at least he fails while daring greatly. So that his place shall never be with those cold and timid souls who know neither victory nor defeat."

Remember push forward in faith and like I said in a previous chapter, maybe you need to add prayer to your list of things to do to ensure success in eliminating your debt.

Chapter Four:
Step Three: Short-Term Savings, How to Plan For Your Near Term Purchases

Now that you understand how to increase your cash flow and how to properly manage your financial resources, let's look at how to purchase those things that you are in need of without using debt instruments to do so.

As part of setting up your financial plan utilizing the Real Wealth Success Formula's seven-step program, which is being outlined within this book, you will need to slowly start implementing each step into your plan as you are able. That means that as you free up resources you will need to allocate a certain amount to other areas of the plan. This will create balance in your life and begin to stabilize your future.

Let's say that you foresee that you will have to soon replace your washer because it is getting old. Since you recognize that the replacement is eminent, planning now for the eventual replacement will benefit you. Start by identifying the washer that you would like to have and sit down and do the math. Determine what you need to put away every month in order to pay for the washer using cash. Make the necessary adjustments to your monthly forecast and start putting it away.

Example: Bill and Mary want to purchase a new refrigerator. The one that they have is several years old and is not cooling as well as it should, not to mention that it is not very energy efficient and they want the additional savings from a more energy efficient model. They go to their local appliance store and find a nice unit for $987. They return home and determine that they would like to replace the unit as soon as possible so they review their monthly forecast. They see that they can allocate $50 a month towards the eventual purchase and make the necessary adjustments. In eighteen months, they purchase their new refrigerator.

This money can be put into a regular savings account since it must remain liquid. I would suggest finding a Credit Union with an interest-bearing account and put your money in there, you might as well earn interest on the money while you are saving. Once you have the specified amount saved up, make the purchase. While you are saving keep your eyes open for the item to go on sale. Maybe you can purchase it sooner and save money in the process.

Every major purchase that you need to make should be done in this manner; especially those items that are not essential like boats, ATV's, etc. There is no valid reason that can be given to substantiate a claim as to why any "toy" should be purchased on credit.

This step doesn't just apply to major purchases; it applies to all forecasted purchases necessary through the year. You know at the beginning of the year that every person in your family is going to have a birthday, you will have an anniversary, Christmas will come again at the end of the year, etc. You can prepare for this by making a specified allocation each month to be used for these events and occasions. None of these should ever catch you unprepared and having to put the purchases on a credit card or other credit instrument.

One of the biggest problems that I've seen in my career are those individuals who every Christmas take out a signature loan at their Credit Union or Bank to purchase gifts. They stress about it all year and never learn to plan for it. They are continuously cycling into debt for an unnecessary reason.

Granted, the typical working person can't necessarily plan the purchase of a home or some vehicles in this manner, but you can save to ensure a substantial down payment to enable you to pay off the debt faster. And if you're disciplined enough you can save up for vehicle purchases in this manner, you just have to be willing to settle for a used vehicle and not a new one. It just takes proper planning and once again discipline and you can completely eradicate any need for debt in your life.

As you set up your finances following this model you will be able to continue to eliminate debt as you started in the previous step because you won't be adding to it as you go. This will add to your peace of mind through the course of the year and you will notice an improvement in your mental, emotional and physical state.

Don't be fooled by all the advertising selling a payment. Insist on knowing the price, the final out the door price. Creditors are tricky they get you with their catchy ad campaigns enticing you with low payments or low interest. They tell you that you can even go 90-days or longer without a payment, but there are always caveats to these programs.

Don't get lulled into a false sense of security or complacency; be wise with your money. You work hard for it, make it work hard for you.

Now, let's take a quick look at credit cards. I've been asked by several people as to whether they should have credit cards or not, or if there is any time that they can be useful—like for example to build credit.

Credit cards have their place in the financial world. They are instruments that can be very useful if proper self-control can be exercised. There are many card companies that offer cash back bonus rewards if you use their card. These cards can be utilized to make money for purchases that you know that you have to make, and that you've properly forecasted and budgeted for. For example, let's say you budget $300 every month for fuel costs, if you have a cash back bonus program on your card (preferably one that pays a higher amount for fuel purchases) use that card and make money on the purchase. Just make sure that you pay off the card every month and never carry a balance on it. You can use this same strategy with Christmas shopping, going out on dates, etc. You just need to make sure that you do not carry a balance on the card. Use the card to make money for yourself, not the card issuer. Do this, and yes, there is a place for credit cards in your financial plan.

Chapter Five:
Step Four: Plan For An Emergency

Planning for an emergency can literally save you financially. Too many Americans in today's society neglect this most import step in financial planning, and when an emergency strikes they turn to that plastic emergency fund that we all carry in our wallets and purses. That's right, today in America the number one "financial instrument" for funding emergencies is our credit card. This has created soaring levels of debt in America's households.

As with the previous step you will need to analyze your annual and monthly forecasts to determine what amount can be allocated towards your emergency fund. Once you've determined a specified amount that will allow you to still maintain adequate levels of funding in the other areas of your financial plan you will need to make the necessary adjustments to the plan.

Planning out what is needed can be tricky since there are many variables involved and we never know when an emergency will strike or what type of an emergency will occur. The best rule of thumb is to plan around insurance deductibles. Find out if you have an insurance deductible which must be met for surgery or hospital benefits, as well as auto and homeowner's deductibles and determine an average amount and begin with this.

> **Example:** Bill and Mary decide that they are ready now to begin funding their emergency fund. They review their insurance policies and find that their auto deductible is $500. They also have a $1,000 homeowner's deductible and a $6000 medical benefits deductible through his employer's health insurance policy. They add these together and determine the average. This is the amount needed to ensure that they can meet an emergency more prepared.
>
> $$\$1000$$
> $$\$500$$
> $$+\$6000$$
> $$\$7500/3 = \$2500$$

Unlike your savings in step three you should consider placing the funds for your emergency fund into a Credit Union that is enough of a distance from your home to ensure that you don't have ready access to the funds. I've seen too often with clients that when they put the funds into a readily available account the big screen television on sale for 50% off the normal price is an emergency. If you want a new big screen television, plan for the purchase and when you find it on sale you already have the money there for the purchase, this is hardly an emergency and therefore you shouldn't utilize these funds in such a flippant manner.

You may even consider using a Money Market Account with check writing privileges to store these funds. Before doing this, you need to determine the minimum permitted withdrawal from the account. Many Money Markets with check writing privileges have minimum withdrawals of $200 or more, which would not benefit you if you were to have an emergency that only cost you $100. Do your homework before institutionalizing your Emergency Fund.

In addition to planning around your insurance deductibles, you will need to plan for financial upheaval in your life, like the loss of employment, injury or sickness, which prohibits you from working. What will your family do if you were to lose your income tomorrow? If you were to lose your job, how long would it take you to find a new one? Many experts have said that it is recommended that you have at least the equivalent of six months' income saved up to maintain your financial stability during a time of unemployment. I myself would go as far as saying that the minimum should be one year's worth of hard expenses saved up for periods of unemployment, especially if your skills are specialized in a specific industry.

What do I mean by hard expenses? These are the expenses that you know that you will have no matter what happens, like mortgage payments, car payments, gas, etc. Other expenses that you know you'll have, like cell phones, utilities, cable or satellite TV, etc. can be adjusted or you can find assistance to help cover them. I would suggest that if you have credit cards that offer credit insurance that you sign up for this service. This will help free up some financial resources and protect your credit.

You know that you need a home to live in, and a car to use while you look for employment, so you need to ensure that you can maintain these within your control during this time. You will need to determine what can be put away on a monthly basis to assist you with putting together the entire amount that you need. In the next chapter we will talk about proper protection, or insurance. There are insurance instruments that can be utilized to help with this step if the unemployment is caused by illness or injury, but they should not be your only source of income since they will only pay 66.5% of your monthly income, and if you are able to live effectively off that you are doing better than you think.

Emergency preparedness doesn't end with putting away money. You need to create a food storage program for your family or yourself if you don't have a family. Begin by storing the basics that you know will assist in maintaining a healthy balance for a period of time. You will eventually need to build this storage up to cover the basics for a year; but start with 3 days and work your way up from there.

The reason why you should start with a 3-day supply is that in the event of an emergency or natural disaster it will take government and public resources about that time to organize and begin distributing needed supplies to survivors. You don't want your family to suffer during this time, so prepare yourself for these types of disasters.

Whether it be a fire, which seems to be very common now days, or a tornado or other type of natural disaster; they can strike when you least expect it, be prepared to care for the basic needs of your family in these occasions.

Look at the situation with Hurricane Katrina, the chaos and turmoil that ensued in the aftermath of that disaster is exactly what you're trying to avoid happening to your family. Have an emergency plan in place for you and your family. Set up a central contact point outside your State of residence that if you are separated all you need do is call that central point and get updates on your family members that are separated from you.

Keep an emergency survival kit in your car and if possible in your office or place of employment. Talk to your employer about providing storage in his/her facility to accommodate emergency supplies for the employees.

Meet with your children's school Principle and find out if there is a plan to ensure that your children will have sufficient supplies if a catastrophe were to occur while they are in school and it is impossible or difficult to evacuate them from the school premises.

Planning never hurt anybody, but not having a plan in place has hurt plenty of people.

In 2017, Hurricane Harvey hit the Houston area in Texas. The destruction was immense. I have a nephew who lives with his family there in the Houston area. He lost pretty much everything to the hurricane. While he was trying to evacuate his family, the waters came upon them and they had to abandon their vehicle and walk for hours in the waist high water. When they finally were "rescued" and placed in a shelter, they didn't have any water or food. His young son was wet, hungry and cold, but there was nothing that could be done.

He got in touch with his father in Washington State who in turn contacted me. I was asked to use resources that are available to me due to my Ecclesiastical responsibilities and see if I could arrange for someone to help my nephew. I was able to locate the local Ecclesiastical leader of the area who immediately assigned someone to go and find him. The person took him and his family into their home and gave them food and a place to stay until they were eventually forced to evacuate the area. The purpose of me relating this story is to reinforce the concept of planning for emergencies. If you have a 72-hour emergency kit you will be able to provide at least the basic needs for your family.

Planning for an emergency should be the focus of every individual. You need to maintain stability for not only yourself and your mental state, but if you have children; your children need stability. Your family needs to know that things will be okay, and planning helps with that.

If you knew that if you were to lose your job tomorrow you'd still be able to eat for at least 6 months, your mind would be at ease with this knowledge. You could focus on finding employment and not worry about your family. Likewise, if you have a job which takes you away from home and you hear while out of town that a natural disaster hit your home area, your mind would be more at ease if you had an emergency plan in place for your family and you would be able to get updates by having that central contact point. Planning is important, so just do it.

Don't get overwhelmed. You don't need to have these funds set up overnight. You must prepare at a pace that ensures overall stability. Remember the analogy of the failed business; if you try to grow too fast without regards for the financial resources available you'll fail even though your intensions were good. Just start with the basics and go from there.

Chapter Six:
Step Five: Proper Protection, Insurance and Even More Insurance

All the planning in the world won't help if you don't think about ensuring the proper protection of your economic value. Each and every person has an economic value attached to him or her, and this value has to be protected. The way this is achieved is through insurance. That's right insurance, that much avoided topic, and I am not just talking about life insurance.

I won't spend too much time reviewing this subject, due to the fact that I'm a licensed Insurance Producer and can get penalized for a potential perceived solicitation of services outside my licensed jurisdiction, but what I will do is describe the various forms of insurance that are needed and their overall benefit to the financial plan.

Life Insurance: If you meet with the standard Insurance Agent you will be told that you should have ten times your annual income in insurance. For some people this is adequate for others it is too much and for still others too little. The problem is that insurance is a sales industry, and the more people that you meet the greater the potential for income. Don't get me wrong I like to make money too, but not at the expense of the individual. To me the calculation is a little more complex than ten times the annual income.

You have to take into consideration the decrease in household expenses with the loss of the individual. The person purchasing the insurance needs to determine what he wants to achieve with the purchase of the insurance policy. To determine the amount of insurance that you will need, ask yourself the following questions:

1. Do you want to provide an education for your children? If so how much of an education and to what school?
2. Are there any foreseeable repairs, which will be needed in your home or vehicles? For example, how old is the roof of your home, will it need to be replaced, or maybe new appliances or a new furnace?
3. Do you want your spouse to return to work and place your children in daycare? Many families face what I call the death of the family unit when the principle breadwinner dies, because the remaining parent needs to make up the loss of income and the children never see the parent. If you decide to provide for the family until the children are grown, until what age will you provide for?
4. What debts are you going to provide for to be paid off by the proceeds of the policy?
5. What is your economic value? This is where you need to really do some thinking. Your economic value is more than just the income that you bring home, what do you do around the house which would otherwise cost money to be done by a third party. There is a website called Salary.com which

has an economic value calculator which you could use to determine the value of your life to your family.

Next, if you or your spouse is a stay-at-home parent what is their economic value? I've met with many clients who when asked the question of determining the economic value of their stay-at-home spouse respond that there is no perceived value economically in the spouse that needs to be protected since they don't bring in an income anyway. There can be nothing further from the truth. Actually, in many instances the stay-at-home parent has a greater value economically than the parent who works away from the home. To see an illustration of this you can visit Salary.com and run the Homemaker economic evaluator (Mom's salary wizard), that they have on their site, you will be surprised.

In other words, if you are a home-maker or a stay at home parent don't get caught up in the erroneous idea that you have no worth because you do. In my own case I'd be lost without the hard work of my beloved companion and helpmeet. She is wonderful, and no amount of money in the world could compensate for her loss to my family.

When looking into purchasing a life insurance policy you need to determine your overall objective, and you need to determine whether or not you know when you will eventually pass away. That's right, because if you purchase a 20-year term policy will you see the benefit of the policy before it expires? If your intention is just to have something cover the cost of the home, don't buy a straight term policy; purchase what is known as a mortgage protection policy. This policy gradually gets smaller as you pay off your home mortgage since it is there to cover the mortgage.

If you want to plan for the long term and ensure that your family is taken care of whether you die tomorrow or when you are 80 years old, then purchase a permanent insurance policy. Even these policies come in a plethora of options. You have whole life, universal life; equity indexed universal life (EIUL), variable universal life, and so forth.

A competent insurance agent will be able to assist you with the right policy for you. If they know off the top of their head, meaning that you tell them that you are interested in a permanent policy and they pull out an application and start filling it out before knowing what you are looking to do with it, RUN! In most cases they are going to try and sell you a straight whole life policy and although whole life it good, it has its uses; and that is typically as final expense insurance and not as a primary insurance policy.

Life insurance is more than just to pay off debts in case you pass away. Life insurance is used a lot in estate planning to help cover expected taxes on the estate. This frees up the estate from having to cover the taxes and allows for the free transfer of the estate to the heirs. Insurance can also be used to fund Trusts at the death of the insured. These Trusts are called Irrevocable Life Insurance Trusts. They can be used to fund a plethora of causes at the death of the insured.

In some cases, people buy life insurance just to cover funeral expenses to alleviate the cost from family members. A typical funeral today can cost $10,000 in some cases. A final expense policy is handy when meeting with the funeral director. Funeral directors are sales people, if you go in with a $500,000 policy they will say that is about right to cover the expense for the funeral. Of course, I am being facetious, but the point is that final expense policies ensure that a proper amount is spent and gives the insured control over the amount spent on his or her funeral.

For business owners, life insurance can be utilized to ensure the continuation of the business if a partner were to pass away. For example, let's say that you have two friends that start a business together. They are the business professionals, not their spouses, but if one were to pass away the remaining partner will find himself or herself in business with the spouse. The remaining partner can't pay off the spouse so therefore they find themselves doing a lot of the work, for the same share as before.

This can be resolved by putting a buy/sell agreement together with insurance as the funding source. That means that the policy is on the partner and the other partner or business entity is the owner of the policy. The policy is attached to a contract which indicates that the money will go to the living spouse of the deceased thus paying them off and freeing up the company from "dead weight".

Another use of insurance in business is through what is called key person policies. These are used to cover the business if they were to lose a key person to the success of the business. This can be top management or even top employees who perform essential duties for the company, who if lost would cause detriment to the business. For example, if a company has a sales person who produces 80% of the sales of the company, they would want to insure this individual. That way if the individual passes away they can use the insurance proceeds to cover the loss in sales until a new person can be found to fill the position and trained to achieve the level of sales lost.

There are many more applications of life insurance in a financial plan. I could go on forever, but I will leave off with this, life insurance is an important element in any plan. I would strongly suggest and urge you to investigate purchasing insurance from your agent and making sure that the agent reviews your policies with you on no less than on an annual basis. Life is constantly changing, and you should make sure that your policies reflect that change.

Disability Insurance: This often-overlooked insurance is probably one of the more necessary insurance policies available to protect the economic stability of the household. People always assume that if something happens they will probably die and that is where the life insurance is needed.

The statistical information available tells quite a different story. It is said that 3 in 5 people will experience a disability in their life extending beyond 2 years. Let's put it this way if you were driving down the street in your neighborhood and saw that three of every five homes were on fire wouldn't you rush home to make sure that you had adequate fire protection for your home, just in case? Yet so many of us don't even consider this an option when considering insurance coverage.

I call disability double death because if you die, you're gone, and you are no longer a financial drain to the assets of the household, if you're disabled though, you are no longer financially benefiting the family, yet you are still a financial drain thus placing your family in a situation where they are worse off because you didn't adequately prepare.

As stated in the previous chapter this insurance doesn't pay everything, and you shouldn't be complacent thinking that it will. The commercials put out by the insurance company that uses the duck as it's mascot, makes it seem that if you are disabled and can't work don't worry they will take care of everything. True they will take care of some items, but they won't take care of everything.

Additionally, when looking at disability insurance you must keep in mind that there are two types of insurance short-term and long-term. Long-term disability coverage has a specified waiting period before it will kick in and start paying usually around 60 to 90 days. You can use short-term disability to bridge this gap. There are many companies which offer a direct pay policy if short-term disability insurance is not offered as part of your employer's benefit package.

Long-Term Care: Long-term care insurance is another type of insurance most often ignored by the consumer. Nobody wants to think about having to be confined to a LTC facility, but it happens 3 of 5 times for a period lasting longer than 2 years. Many people just figure that their family will take care of them. They neglect to realize that if they are disabled and unable to do anything the individual who supposedly will be taking care of them is working therefore unable to provide the care needed.

Or maybe you're one of those who believes that LTC insurance is for seniors, and therefore you will look into it when you get closer to retirement. Although the majority of those consumers who own LTC insurance are seniors it is not merely for them. Begin to start planning on securing LTC during a period in your life when it will be the least expensive, once you're older it will be expensive just like any insurance program available for the senior market.

Not all long-term care policies require that you stay in a nursing home or assisted living facility. They do provide for in-home care for those who desire this type of care. This will allow your family to help and when they need a break, they can turn to the policy to cover the expense of having someone come in. You will need to make sure that your policy provides for this method of care.

Some policies will payout a specified amount of money regardless of what is paid in actual expenses, and some will only pay actual expenses. If you have questions please speak to a competent agent, and I would suggest speaking to a few agents to ensure that you get a competent one to work with and not what I call a body stacker just looking for numbers and not at all interested in providing service to the client.

Voluntary or Ancillary Insurance: These are typically health-underwritten policies, which cover non-covered health expenses. The leading policy in this genre of insurance is Cancer Insurance. These policies cover expenses not covered by your health insurance carrier in the event that you should be diagnosed with cancer. According to the American Cancer Society, Americans have a 1 in 3 chance of being diagnosed with cancer and about two thirds of the expenses are not covered by insurance. These expenses are deductibles, co-pays, insurance limitations, household living expenses, travel expenses, etc.

Cancer Insurance helps the individual pay for these expenses and helps maintain the household and replace lost income in some cases. They are essential in protecting the assets of your estate to ensure financial continuity while you are facing this dreaded disease.

Other policies that fall within this genre are Accident Policies, Hospitalization Policies, Specified Disease Policies, etc. They all work in much the same way as the Cancer policy and can be effective in each their own way.

Then of course you have your auto, homeowners, health, liability, etc., which everyone should have and maintain current. The common thread with all insurance is that it is a stop loss. Insurance ensures that your financial assets will not be diminished in the event of an unforeseen accident or untimely death or sickness.

Insurance is important and should seriously be considered in the maintaining of a strong and viable financial plan. I would suggest speaking with various agents until you find one who has your best interest in mind and is not trying to sell you the one product that his marketing agency has informed him that he must sell. Make sure that they work with you to ensure that your coverage is adequate and within your allotted budget, of course you may need to incrementally increase coverage's as your financial means increase, but any good agent worth your business should be performing annual reviews with you to ensure that your coverage is still adequate for your family's needs.

Chapter Seven:
Step Six: Long-Term Savings, Because You Do Want To Retire

No matter where you live or what level of financial success you've achieved, there is one thing that everybody longs for, and this is retirement. That phase in your life where you no longer have to worry about working and all you need to do is have fun. Then why do so many people return to work after retiring? The difficultly involved with retirement is outliving or the fear of outliving your retirement savings. Whether you depend on a pension, annuity, or 401k eventually the money will dry up. The paradigm is causing more and more people to continue working beyond the normal retirement age to try and save more money.

The problem is that we have all been told that we should put money into IRA's, 401k's, annuities, CD's, etc., but we are not taught what to do with that money once it is time to start using it. Unfortunately, a concise treatment of this subject would take up an entire book of its own, so I will briefly discuss the importance of properly saving and distributing your savings.

First, let's cover the savings aspect of this step since that is where the majority of you are at this time. Let me start by debunking the myth that a good and secure method to save for retirement is a CD (Certificate of Deposit). There could be nothing further from the truth.

If you take and illustrate the rate of return or interest yield of this financial instrument you will see that over the course of 25 years you actually earn a negative rate of return, you may have more money than what you started out with, but a completely weaker buying power. To determine actual rate of return you have to look at all factors not just interest yields. You must consider inflation, cost of living, and taxes. If the average CD pays a percentage yield of .5%, and inflation increases at a rate of 3% per annum and the cost of living index increases at the same rate, then you have a 20% Capital Gains Tax to pay, where are your gains? In my opinion you should only use CD's for temporary gains utilizing the introductory rates offered by some banks and then quickly move them into other accounts. Never hold your funds in a CD for a period longer than 6 months.

Next, we will combine IRA's, annuities, and 401k's, since they are all annuities just regulated by different laws. These are all viable instruments to use for your retirement savings. IRA's allow you to put your money away and defer taxes until a future date, when your taxable income will be less (in theory). The problem with deferring your taxes is that you will no longer have any write offs with which to decrease your effective tax rate, which may or may not put you into an unfavorable tax bracket depending on your draw and maintainable income during retirement. The government seeing the hesitation in some Americans to utilize IRA's created a second-generation IRA called the ROTH. The

ROTH allows the individual to pay taxes now and not pay taxes on gains, which enables you to pay on current taxable income while you still have your deductions in place. There is one caveat to this, the rules creating the ROTH state that at any future date the rules can change, and future growth can be taxed if deemed necessary. The rules governing ROTH IRA's have changed several times since their inception, and we can rest assured that they will continue to change especially in today's economy.

The 401k works in a similar manner as the IRA, but since it is employer sponsored you have the luxury in many instances to have a company match (not all companies do this, but there are many who do). This basically translates into free money going into your account and growing to benefit you at retirement. Other than this there is no real difference between the 401k and IRA accounts.

There are many different types of annuities available to the consumer. Basically, all that an annuity is, is an agreement between the annuitant (you) and the insurance company, contracting to provide income payments to the annuitant at a future date to be specified by the contract owner in return for specified payments to be made to the insurance company. These payments are placed into various accounts depending on the type of annuity chosen and grow in accordance with the market or guaranteed interest rate.

The three main types of annuities are fixed, variable and equity indexed, and can be explained as follows:

Fixed: The contract specifies a fixed interest rate that you are promised which will be credited to the portion of your payment which is placed into the cash value portion of the annuity contract.

Variable: The contract provides various sub-accounts, which are professionally managed accounts usually Mutual Funds, Money Markets, and fixed accounts. Premium payments are placed into these sub-accounts and grow or lose with the market. You are able to choose the accounts that you want based upon the risk tolerance that you have.

Equity-Indexed: These are my particular favorite. They give you the benefits of a variable type product in that they increase in value with the market fixed to a particular index and have guarantees associated with them so that if the market experiences no gains you are still guaranteed an increase in your account. The best feature of these annuities is that most of them have what is called a high-water mark. This allows you to keep the gains that are credited to your account even though the market decreases; you never lose your accumulated cash value.

In addition to these financial instruments you have various other investment accounts that can be used to produce retirement income. It is essential that you thoroughly investigate any and all potential investments; including annuities to ensure that they are viable products and especially that the investment is a legal investment product. Too many people are relieved of their life savings due to investment scams every year. The rule of thumb is that if it sounds too good to be true, it probably is. Be especially aware of investments that offer a high interest yield. Most of these programs are highly illegal in the United States. In my line of work, I deal with aspiring business owners all the time as I work with them writing their business plans, consulting with them and helping them find funding for their ventures. When dealing with potential investors about 90% of the time I am dealing with crooked individuals. They want lots of money and guarantee the world, but after deeper interrogation they are uncovered for what they are. Lucky for my clients I am a Private Investigator with a specialty in working fraud and have studied the art of interrogation. I've saved my clients thousands upon thousands of dollars by protecting them from unsavory individuals and their investment scams.

Several types of investment strategies or vehicles that can be used for retirement are as follows:

Corporate Stocks: Simple enough, you purchase shares of ownership into a company, your money grows as the company grows and diminishes as the company struggles. Dividends are typically paid out on stocks and paid directly to the stockholder via cash payout or in some cases additional stock.

Mutual Funds: You've heard the adage of not putting your eggs in one basket? Mutual funds follow the same philosophy in that they spread the risk over several companies by buying stock in these entities. Some are industry specific while others invest in performing companies throughout the market. Since the inception of Mutual funds there has not been a fund that has gone under, not even during the Depression. These funds range from high risk to minimal risk and your investing in one of these accounts will depend on your risk tolerance.

Bonds: Unlike stocks, bonds are the purchase of debt shares of a company. You take upon yourself the duty to assist in paying off certain debts that the company has secured and in return they offer you a percentage increase of your investment at the termination of the term of the bond. With bonds you take upon yourself the risk that the company will go under and be unable to make good on the bond. The most common type of bonds are Municipal Bonds, they are normally considered very secure since you are investing into municipalities but pay more often than not a very small return on the investment. The historical idea that Municipal Bonds are secure has been shattered with the trend of Municipalities going bankrupt, for example Detroit, MI, and Hartford, CT is teetering on the precipice of bankruptcy as well.

With any investment the gains that you realize are dependent upon the risk that you are willing to take. The higher the risk the higher the potential gains, and vice-verse the lower the risk the smaller the yield. It is wise to be more aggressive while you are younger and have the ability to lose in the market and still be able to recover any losses before retirement. As you get older your risk tolerance should decrease in order to stabilize your funds to ensure a timely retirement.

The most overlooked aspect of retirement planning is the distribution phase. You are left alone in many instances to determine how to utilize your retirement accounts and end up having to pay higher taxes and or returning to work because your funds expire before you do.

Proper distribution planning varies from individual to individual and a competent financial advisor should be sought to determine how to structure the payout phase of your retirement.

As a basic structure you should have your retirement distributed in more than one type of account. This means that you should not only utilize a 401k, but that you should have a 401k and maybe one or two additional annuities or trade accounts that you manage and maintain.

If you can count on receiving a portion of the social security program, determine how much you will be receiving, plan on what type of lifestyle you are expecting to live during your retirement and draw from your accounts appropriately. If you have annuities I would urge you not to annuitize the account unless you absolutely have to. Leave at least one account to continue to grow so that you can burn through the others first all the while continuing to increase the value of the remaining unused account.

Another method used by seniors is the use of reverse mortgages. Traditionally reverse mortgages have been detrimental to seniors, but the emergence of the HECM (Home Equity Conversion Mortgage) works well for seniors to produce the needed funds for retirement, and you keep ownership of your home. I would suggest speaking with competent advisors before entering into any reverse mortgage program. If they are not planned right they can be more harmful than helpful to the senior and their family.

Your best bet would be to meet with someone who specializes in senior issues, there is a designation issued by the financial industry to those who have completed courses and proved proficiency via testing which designates the individual as a certified senior planning specialist. They should be able to assist you in implementing a proper distribution of your retirement funds.

Again, I cannot stress enough the importance of working with honest individuals and to do your background work on any individual or program before doing anything with regards to your retirement savings. Seniors are targets to criminals, and they try to use fear tactics or pie in the sky promises to get your money. One of the most used tactics against seniors is becoming a friend or gaining trust through dishonest means. A good movie to watch that depicts a true story wherein this takes place is called "_Polka King_" starring Jack Black. The moral of this is basically, don't be a victim, stay in charge of your retirement future. Always seek the advice and counsel of a competent advisor prior to making any moves with your retirement funds.

Chapter Eight:
Step Seven: Plan Your
Estate On Any Income

Traditionally when people think of estate planning they think of the rich creating their trusts and endowments protecting their massive homes and large-scale assets. The average blue-collar worker has been overlooked because their assets don't exceed $1,000,000. Estate planning is expensive, isn't it? You have to hire lawyers and financial planners and accountants, it's just so complicated that families with little "tangible" assets and liquid wealth are not encouraged to prepare their estates for proper distribution when the estate owner passes.

Actually, this view of estate planning is only a small portion of what planning your estate entails. Every family has an estate. An estate can be defined as accumulated assets of a perceived value. If you have children and a spouse, you have an estate that needs to be protected.

Part of your Estate Plan is your Living Will/Advance Directives. A Living Will directs what you would have done with your "estate" in the event that you are injured and remain living but in a state of suspended consciousness and are unable to direct the affairs of your estate yourself. What would happen to your children if you and your spouse were to be injured and unable to direct what should be done for their care? Do you trust anyone to take them and care for them, or do you trust the courts to properly direct what should happen to them if there is no close relative that can take responsibility for them in a timely manner? What of your house payments and other debt service, who is to take the lead of these to ensure that they are properly taken care of? Who is going to speak on your behalf?

In connection to your Living Will and Advance Directives, you should consider a Power of Attorney. Choose an individual whom you trust and designate them with an executable Power of Attorney to act in your behalf. You will need someone authorized to handle your business affairs to avoid a cessation caused by any legal hold up or loophole in your authorizing documents. If you can't speak for yourself, you need to have someone able and willing to speak for you.

Advanced Directives let the medical professionals know what you want done if something were to happen to you. Do you remember the Terry Shivo case in Florida a number of years ago? The court battles that ensued because the husband wanted his wife taken off of life-support, and her parents endeavored in vain to stop it. They both claimed to know the desires of Mrs. Shivo, ultimately the husband won, and she was allowed to expire. The presence of Advanced Directives eliminates the confusion as to what your desires are. It is important to note that the preparation of a Living Will and Advanced Directives is useless unless they are assessable, and someone knows where to find them. There are programs available online that allows you to securely store information such as this online and which makes the information available when needed. The only problem is letting people know that you have the service and carrying the appropriate card with login information. Whatever you decide to do, you need to ensure that someone knows where you keep your Advanced Directives and Living Will.

In addition to the Living Will and Advance Directives you will need to prepare your Last Will and Testament. Typically, a lawyer will charge anywhere from $500 to $25,000 depending on the size of estate and work done to prepare it. Many people who are living from paycheck to paycheck are unable to pay this much for the preparation of their Will and therefore many people die in testate, which means that you die without having prepared a Will. In today's Internet age there are alternatives to using a lawyer for the preparation of Will's. There are many sites available which can prepare your Will for a minimal fee. Having said this, I am not endorsing any particular site, but I encourage you to do your homework and make sure that the Will that you have prepared is a legal document in the state that you live in. You don't want to pay good money and have it contested in court successfully.

If you are a member of Pre-paid Legal one of your benefits is the free preparation of a Will by an attorney. I would strongly encourage you to utilize this service, and to have it reviewed and updated annually. Once again, I am not endorsing Pre-paid Legal, I am merely informing you as a consumer on what avenues you can take to prepare a Will, which will protect your family. Additionally, they get upset when I tell people to sign up get the free Will and then cancel the service. It is the cheapest and most effective method to use to get a well-written Will.

The most in-expensive method to use in the preparation of a Will would be a Do-It-Yourself kit that you can purchase at any local office- supply store like Office Depot. These kits provide pre-typed forms, with blanks where you are to fill your particular information into. Make sure that you get the document notarized when you are completed with it. This way you can be sure that the contestability of the document will be lessened.

Speaking of contestability, any document even those prepared by attorneys can be contested in court, but the presence of a Will greatly reduces estate hold ups in the court system. When an estate owner passes away, those individuals who benefit from the disbursement of the estate are in a highly emotional state. The existence of a Will, Advance Directives, Living Will, etc., will greatly aid in the transition period wherein business needs to move forward. Peace of mind is what is needed during this time period.

As you build your wealth and increase your assets you will need to take your Estate Plan further. A good Estate Plan is reviewed annually and adjustments for life's changing elements are included to ensure adequate coverage of all aspects relating to your estate and most importantly your family.

I've spoken to many people who have a Will, but it was written more than 10 years previous. Their lives had changed, but their Will never did. It was obsolete and would not have provided adequate protection for their then current family situations. I can't stress enough that every aspect of your financial plan should be reviewed annually with your financial, tax and legal advisor. Never leave anything to chance. Most people update their vehicle more often than they update their financial plan. We as a Nation have to move away from this trend and work hard to ensure financial solvency through all phases of life.

Chapter Nine: The Most Common Denominator of the Formula

If I am to keep up with the analogy of a formula, since I call this program the Real Wealth Success Formula, I need to explain the most common denominator. This principle is not one of the seven steps, but it is the most common element found in each one, and that is faith. As a matter of fact, faith is a motivating force that pushes us along the way. Faith gives us hope for a positive outcome even when we can't see it. Many people shy away from talking about God, and His ability to help His children. They want to keep things "professional", or maybe they are afraid of "offending" those who might not believe in God. If you don't believe in God, I'm sorry. Now understand that I am not sorry for bringing Him up, but I am sorry that you have not yet realized that God is a major source of success in any venture. He wants you to be happy and successful.

The Formula for success can be written out as follows:

$$\frac{\text{Hard Work (Seven Steps)}}{\text{(Faith + Prayer)}} = \text{Success}$$

I have met with countless individuals during the course of my career and have put together many customized financial plans. It took me awhile to understand this common denominator though. In the beginning of my career when clients would fail, I would just chock it up to failure on their part, and indeed it was; but not as you would think. After a while of seeing some clients succeed and other just outright failing and struggling to make the plan work; I started asking a question of all my clients regardless of their individual beliefs, "Are you paying an honest tithe?" Pretty simple, huh? Without fail every client who was failing at his or her plan would answer, either "what's that" or "no". Nobody ever said yes. Those who did were succeeding and making headway in their plans. I started building this aspect into my plans and encouraging my clients to follow through so that they could succeed.

There is a scripture that I love found in the Bible, in the Book of Malachi. It reads, "Will a man rob God? Yet ye have robbed me. But ye say, wherein have we robbed thee? In tithes and offerings." Then comes the kicker, "Bring ye all the tithes into the storehouse, that there may be meat in mine house, and…", just listen to what comes next, "…**prove me now herewith,** saith the Lord of Hosts, if I will not open you the windows of heaven, and pour you out a blessing, that there shall not be room enough to receive it." How many times do we read in the words of God for us to prove Him? We've been given a promise that if we pay our tithes and offerings we will be blessed, and I believe Him. I've proved Him, and I can say that I am a witness to the truthfulness of the words spoken through the mouth of the Prophet Malachi. Even in my most lean financial circumstances I've made sure that the first thing that is paid is my tithing and other offerings that I owe to the Lord for His blessings in my life.

I remember once, we were going through a very difficult financial time. Money was not only scarce, but rare in our account. One day after church services we were approached by the brethren from our Church and asked to provide a donation to help the poor. We normally would provide a certain amount every month. My wife came to me and told me that the amount that we normally gave was all that we had in the account and if we gave we would have nothing to purchase needed groceries. I told her that we would give what we normally would give and that I trusted that God would recompense us ten-fold for our sacrifice. She agreed, and we made the donation.

The following day she went to work and found an envelope on her desk. When she opened it up she found an amount of money representing a ten-fold increase from what we gave. So, do I believe that we are blessed when we look outward rather than inward when it comes to serving others? The answer is yes.

It doesn't matter what church you belong to or even if you don't have a religion. The principle is simple, give of yourself and you will be blessed. Pay your tithes, give offerings, or donate money to charity if you don't have a church that you attend. Call it Karma or whatever you want, I guarantee you that if you do this you will be blessed, and you will have success in establishing your financial plan effectively. Not only that, but you will feel better about yourself. There is a feeling that comes over you when you put other's needs over your own. It is hard to explain. Those who have given of themselves to help others know the feeling, but individuals who never have opened themselves up to do anything for someone else are lost to the sensation that comes from serving our fellow man.

If you are apt to pray, do so and do it often. Include God in the establishing of your plan. When you set your goals at the very beginning be sure to establish spiritual goals as well. You need to remain a well-balanced individual so establish goals based upon the 4 areas of your life, personal, spiritual, career, and family/relationship. Pray over your goals and ask for assistance in meeting them.

In the Bible, the Book of Hosea sixth chapter, sixth verse, we read; "For I desired *mercy*, and not sacrifice; and the knowledge of God more than burnt offerings." In the original Hebrew text, the word found in place of mercy is heced, which basically means the thinking of or the inclusion of intimately. It is similar to the individual who during the course of the day calls their spouse just to tell them that they were thinking of them and wanted to tell them that they loved them out of the blue.

That is what God wants from us, to include Him in our lives and our decisions. Now that is not to say that He will direct us in all things. We come to this earth to further our development and to learn to do His will so that we can return to live with Him in heaven. There are some things that He wants us to figure out, but He will help us find strength during the process of figuring it out.

So basically, what I am saying is that if you want to see true success in your financial and life endeavors include God in your planning and pay your tithes and offerings. Give of yourself to others. Never turn your back on the poor and needy. Serve your fellow men and your community. Stand up for truth. You will do well to always remember the teachings of Jesus Christ, "that which ye have seen me do, go and do thou likewise."

Chapter Ten: Conclusion: No More Excuses, It's Time For A Change

Now that you've been empowered with knowledge, there is nothing holding you back from being able to succeed in life and build real wealth for you and your family, except yourself. The time for procrastination is past, you have to stand tall, square your shoulders, and declare in a firm and determined voice that you can and will do it. Be positive, use positive and empowering self-talk when you discuss your finances with your spouse. If you are at all uncertain about the possibility of success, you will not succeed. Self-talk is powerful, and we need to empower ourselves with good positive language. I remember seeing once a little paper that my wife had taped to our bathroom mirror that simply said, "words have power". They do, they have the power to build and to destroy.

Put your financial house in order and you will see that life will become pleasant. Financial freedom is just that, freedom. As long as you allow yourself to be burdened with debt and continue on with no financial plan or clue you will forever remain in bondage. As a Nation we did away with slavery in the 1800's, yet we are eagerly seeking opportunities to enslave ourselves to new masters today. We readily take upon ourselves more debt, and then complain about our financial resources and our inability to do anything because our paychecks are spent before we even get them. Then we look to the government to save us, and all they will do is enslave you even more with onerous taxes and government interference in your life. You can get rid of debt, but you can't get rid of government.

The mind-set of instant gratification must cease today. As we begin to free ourselves from the shackles of debt, and poverty our Nation will begin to strengthen. Our economy will realize real growth. Inflated numbers produced by purchasing on credit are hollow, and the market and dollar are reflecting that today. Markets can't be more stable than the people propping them up, and in a free market system the consumer is what drives the market.

I understand that you are probably overwhelmed at this point as you think of having to implement each of the Seven Steps outlined in this book. Although the task looks daunting I assure you that you can do it. Just take it one step at a time. Don't go too fast trying to do everything all at once, unless you find that your financial capacity is currently at a level where you can.

If you need assistance you can always contact a competent advisor to assist you in implementing a sound plan that you can live with. If you would like, you can contact my office by emailing me directly at: aramirez@fixmybusiness.net. I am always willing to help where I can. I would also love to hear of your personal experiences associated with the reading of this book and the implementation of these steps in your life.

I wish you the best of luck as you begin a new chapter in your life. One free of fear and uncertainty as you pierce the darkness and see the light of hope spring upon your mind illuminating your understanding to see the benefit of your work and the value of your life, family and freedom. Good luck and God speed. Now go out and get it done!

Appendix:

Guidelines to Preparing Wills

Prepared by NewLine Consulting

In preparing a Will it is important that the laws regarding the legality of the Will for your state of residence be followed. If prepared by a qualified attorney, you will be ensured that the Will is legal and binding in your state. The preparation of a Will can cost up to $25,000, but more cost-effective sources are available in today's online community. You can prepare a state legal Will for anywhere from $10 to $50, it is important to keep an eye out for those sites that would cheat you out of your money and provide a product that is not legal in your state. A more cost-effective approach is to purchase a kit and prepare your Will yourself. It is important to prepare ones will to avoid leaving your estate in testate at your passing.

Following you will find some common sections that should be included in your Will to ensure proper implementation at the time of your passing. NewLine Consulting is not endorsing or encouraging any particular Will preparation site or kit. We do encourage whenever possible that our clients utilize a qualified attorney in the preparation of their Will.

Common Contents of a Will

Opening:
Identify yourself, county where you reside, and state in which you reside. Proclaim soundness of mind and understanding of intent, and that it is done according to your own free will and not under duress of any outside influence.

Article One:
Marriage and Children- Who are you married to and who are your children with dates of birth

Article Two:
Debts and Expenses- How to dispose of your debts.

Article Three:
Special Bequests of Real and or Personal Property

Article Four:
Homestead or Primary Residence

Article Five:
All Remaining Property- Residuary Clause

Article Six:
Contingent-All Remaining Property- Residuary Clause

Article Seven:
Property to Vest in Trustee or Minor Beneficiary

Article Eight:
Creditors of Beneficiaries

Article Nine:
Appointment of Trustee

Article Ten:
Appointment of Guardian

Article Eleven:
Appointment of Personal Representative, Executor, or Executrix

Article Twelve:
Waiver of Bond, Inventory, Accounting, Reporting and Approval

Article Thirteen:
Powers of Personal Representative, Executor, or Executrix

Article Fourteen:
Construction Intentions- Make sure your intentions in preparing the Will are known. Clear up anything that could be misinterpreted during the execution of the Will.

Article Fifteen:
Misc. Provisions- Make various wishes known (i.e. where do you want to be buried, if somebody mentioned in the will is indebted to you at the time of your passing, etc.).

Closing:
Close your will by signing an affidavit in the presence of two or more witnesses. You may wish to use a Notary of the public as well to ensure proper recognition of your Will. Each witness who signs the Will must list Name, Address and Phone Number, and must sign the affidavit stating that they witnessed the signing of the Will by the Testator and that it was done under their own free will and under no duress from any outside source or individual.

Depending on the number of pages that the Will prepared contains the Testator will need to sign each page on the bottom to verify that the page is an actual document in the complete legal document being implemented.

www.ingramcontent.com/pod-product-compliance
Lightning Source LLC
Chambersburg PA
CBHW071250170526
45165CB00003B/1286